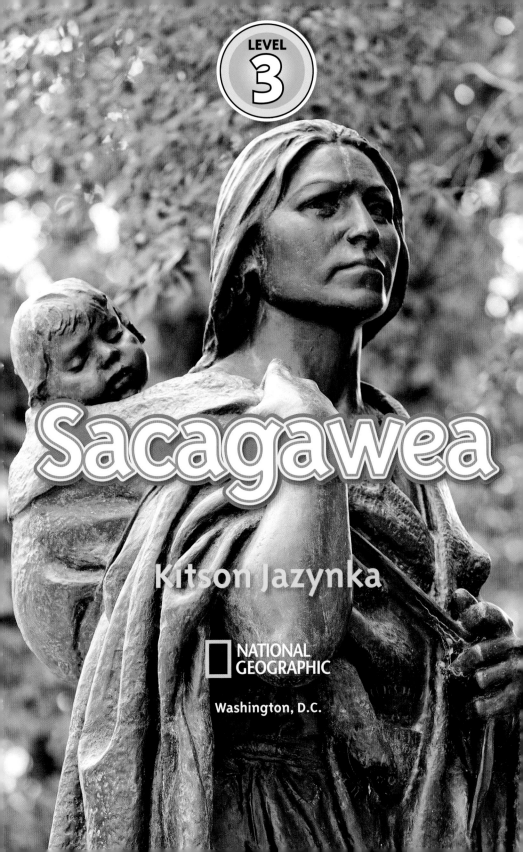

LEVEL 3

Sacagawea

Kitson Jazynka

NATIONAL GEOGRAPHIC

Washington, D.C.

For young explorers everywhere,
especially Max and Quinn. —K.J.

The publisher and author gratefully acknowledge the expert review of this book
by Carolyn Gilman, historian, museum exhibits developer, and author of *Lewis and Clark:
Across the Divide.*

Not much is known about Sacagawea, except the information provided by Lewis, Clark, and other members of the Corps of Discovery. No images of her likeness were made during her lifetime. The photos on pages 4, 17, 22–23, 27, 30, 34, 36, 44, and 45 are from the National Geographic large-format film *Lewis and Clark: Great Journey West* and show modern-day actors playing historic roles. The cover art depicts what Sacagawea might have looked like at age 15, at the time of the expedition.

Paperback ISBN: 978-1-4263-1963-1
Library edition ISBN: 978-1-4263-1964-8

Book design by YAY! Design

cover, Patrick Faricy; 1, Franz-Marc Frei/Corbis; 4, Mark Thiessen/NGS; 7 (UP), David R. Frazier Photolibrary, Inc./Science Source; 7 (LO), Marilyn Angel Wynn/Nativestock/Getty Images; 8, Burstein Collection/Corbis; 9, Tom Bean/Corbis; 10, ileana_bt/Shutterstock; 11, Greg Vaughn/Alamy; 12, Stock Montage/Getty Images; 13, FXQuadro/Shutterstock; 14, GL Archive/Alamy; 16 (LE), James E. Russell/National Geographic Creative; 16 (RT), James E. Russell/National Geographic Creative; 17, John Livzey/National Geographic Television & Film; 18 (UP), Drozdowski/Shutterstock; 18 (LO), Masterfile; 19 (UP), Andreas von Einsiedel/Corbis; 19 (CTR), National Museum of the American Indian, Smithsonian Institution (22/9158); 19 (LO), Hulton Archive/Getty Images; 21, Michael Haynes; 22–23, Lisa Truitt/National Geographic Television & Film; 24, National Museum of American History, Smithsonian Institution; 25 (UP), The Granger Collection, NYC—All rights reserved; 25 (LOLE), North Wind Picture Archives/Alamy; 25 (LORT), North Wind Picture Archives/Alamy; 26, Smithsonian Institution/Corbis; 27, John Livzey/National Geographic Television & Film; 29, Michael Haynes; 30, John Livzey/National Geographic Television & Film; 31, Tupungato/Shutterstock; 33, Ira Block/National Geographic Creative; 33 (INSET), Ira Block/National Geographic Creative; 34, Mark Thiessen/NGS; 36–37 (Background), John Livzey/National Geographic Television & Film; 36 (UPLE), John Livzey/National Geographic Television & Film; 36 (UPRT), Brooklyn Museum/Corbis; 36 (LOLE), James E. Russell/National Geographic Creative; 36 (LOCTR), James E. Russell/National Geographic Creative; 36 (LORT), Vladimir Wrangel/Shutterstock; 37 (UPLE), Ira Block/National Geographic Creative; 37 (UPRT), Tom Reichner/Shutterstock; 37 (CTR); North Wind Picture Archives/Alamy; 37 (LORT), Library of Congress Prints & Photographs Division; 38, Bobby Bank/WireImage/Getty Images; 39 (UP), GraphicaArtis/Corbis; 39 (LOLE), AP Images/Nancy Kuehn; 39 (LORT), Neftali/Shutterstock; 40, steve bly/Alamy; 41, David Lowe/Alamy; 42–43 (beads), age fotostock Spain, S.L/Alamy; 43, Michael Haynes; 44 (UP), Mark Thiessen/NGS; 44 (CTR), Marilyn Angel Wynn/Nativestock/Corbis; 44 (LO), John Livzey/National Geographic Television & Film; 45 (UP), Mark Thiessen/NGS; 45 (CTR RT), John Livzey/National Geographic Television & Film; 45 (CTR LE), Charles Knowles/Shutterstock; 45 (LO), Michael Haynes; 46 (UPRT), Artazum and Iriana Shiyan/Shutterstock; 46 (CTR LE), Glynnis Jones/Shutterstock; 46 (CTR RT), Smithsonian Institution/Corbis; 46 (LOLE), Benoit Tessier/Reuters/Corbis; 46 (LORT), steve bly/Alamy; 47 (UPLE), George W. Bailey/Shutterstock; 47 (UPRT), Steven Kazlowski/Science Faction/Corbis; 47 (CTR RT), Ruskin Photos/Alamy; 47 (LOLE), North Wind Picture Archives/Alamy; 47 (LORT), David R. Frazier Photolibrary, Inc./Alamy; header, Field Museum Library/Getty Images; vocab, Tazzina/iStockphoto

National Geographic supports K–12 educators with ELA Common Core Resources.
Visit natgeoed.org/commoncore for more information.

Printed in the United States of America
14/WOR/1

Table of Contents

Who Was Sacagawea? 4

Growing Up Shoshoni 6

Kidnapped! 8

A Fur Trader's Wife 12

The Corps of Discovery 14

In Her Time 18

The Expedition 20

Quick Thinking 24

Miles and Miles 26

Finding the Shoshoni 28

To the West 30

Mission Complete 32

8 Cool Facts About Sacagawea 36

Her Final Years 38

In Honor of Sacagawea 40

Fact or Fiction? 42

Be a Quiz Whiz! 44

Glossary 46

Index 48

Who Was Sacagawea?

A movie actress as Sacagawea

Sacagawea (Sa-kuh-ga-WEE-uh) was a young Native American woman. She traveled by boat and on foot for more than 2,600 miles.

She and the other courageous explorers camped for more than a year among wild animals like grizzly bears, buffalo, cougars, and wolves. During that expedition (eks-puh-DISH-un) across the United States in the early 1800s, Sacagawea helped make history.

Word to Know

EXPEDITION: A long journey

Growing Up Shoshoni

Sacagawea was a brave explorer. Not much else is known about her life. But historians believe she was born around 1790. Her village (in present-day Idaho) sat in the harsh Rocky Mountains. It was not easy for her Shoshoni or "Snake" Indian people to find food. As a nomadic tribe, the Shoshoni Indians moved between homes to hunt buffalo, wild sheep, salmon, and squirrel.

Sacagawea collected berries, seeds, acorns, and even grasshoppers to help provide food for her family.

Sacagawea's village was near the Salmon River in present-day Idaho.

The Shoshoni people dug up the roots of camas flowers for food.

Words to Know

HISTORIAN: A person who studies history

NOMADIC: Moving around in search of food

Kidnapped!

This drawing of Hidatsa warriors on horseback appears on a painted robe made from buffalo skin.

When Sacagawea was about ten years old, a war party from another tribe attacked her family. Young Hidatsa warriors, out to prove their bravery, captured Sacagawea. They took her to live in their village more than 800 miles away.

It must have been like moving to a foreign city. The Hidatsa lived in villages along the Knife River (in present-day North Dakota). Thousands of people from different tribes lived together. Tree trunks held up large, dome-shaped homes. People spoke different languages, grew crops, and traded furs, buffalo skins, and horses.

The Hidatsa people lived in dome-shaped homes like this one.

In the Knife River Villages, Sacagawea survived by learning a new way of life. She learned a new language. She tended fields in the spring and harvested corn, squash, beans, and prairie turnips in the summer and fall. She made pottery. She watched ceremonies with dancing, colorful clothing, and music. People in this village celebrated many things, such as the harvest and the return of birds that had flown south for the winter.

That's a Fact!

At a historical site in North Dakota, you can visit the village where Sacagawea lived after she was kidnapped.

This model shows what the inside of a Hidatsa home looked like.

A Fur Trader's Wife

Traders would often meet at posts to trade.
This art shows a trading post in Canada.

Fox furs

When Sacagawea was about 15 years old, she married Toussaint Charbonneau (Too-SONT SHAR-bon-oh). He was a French–Canadian fur trader. As a fur trader's wife, Sacagawea met traders from around the world. She even traded on her own for beads, silver, and cloth. Soon she prepared to have a baby.

The Corps of Discovery

In 1803, President Thomas Jefferson made a deal with France that almost doubled the size of the United States. He planned an expedition to explore the territory. He wanted to find a water route to the Pacific Ocean. He called the mission the Corps (CORE) of Discovery.

President Thomas Jefferson

The Louisiana Purchase

In 1803, President Thomas Jefferson made a deal with France for land west of the Mississippi River. This deal was called the Louisiana Purchase. Jefferson paid about three cents an acre for the land. It stretched to the Rocky Mountains.

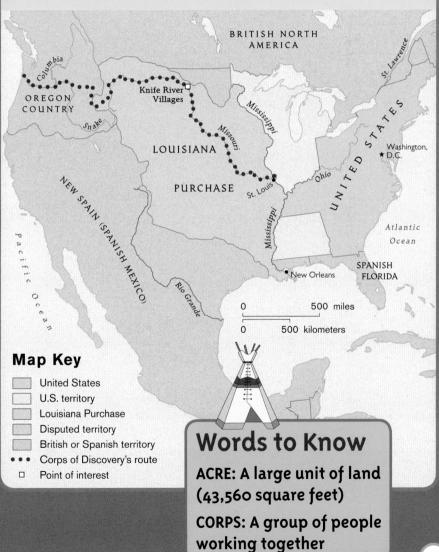

Map Key

■ United States
■ U.S. territory
■ Louisiana Purchase
■ Disputed territory
■ British or Spanish territory
••• Corps of Discovery's route
□ Point of interest

Words to Know

ACRE: A large unit of land (43,560 square feet)

CORPS: A group of people working together

Captain Meriwether Lewis

Captain William Clark

Captain Meriwether Lewis and Captain William Clark led the expedition. In the spring of 1804, they left St. Louis, Missouri, in a keelboat and smaller, wooden boats called pirogues (pee-ROAGS). They traveled through areas including what is now Missouri, Nebraska, Iowa, and South Dakota.

Word to Know

PIROGUE: A small wooden boat

In November, they reached the Knife River Villages and planned to stay for the winter. They set up a camp and called it Fort Mandan.

The Corps spent the winter in present-day North Dakota.

Sacagawea was a young woman in 1804. Many things were different from how they are today.

Food

Instead of shopping for groceries, Indian families grew fruits and vegetables and hunted. They stored food for the winter by drying and smoking meat.

Transportation

Most people traveled on foot or horseback or by boat.

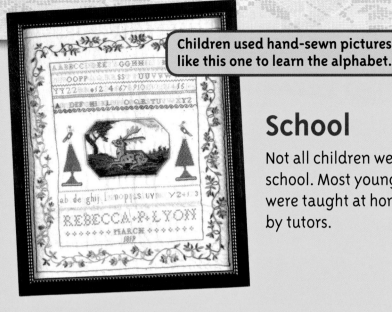

School

Not all children went to school. Most young people were taught at home or by tutors.

Toys and Free Time

Indian children played with dolls, toy bows, and clay. They competed in ball games. In winter they had sleds made out of buffalo ribs.

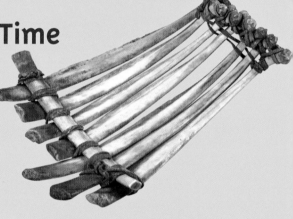

U.S. Events

In 1804, Thomas Jefferson began his second term as president of the United States.

The Expedition

Over the winter, Lewis and Clark hired Charbonneau as an interpreter. They knew he would bring Sacagawea, too. Lewis and Clark needed her because she spoke Shoshoni. She could help them talk with the Shoshoni Indians to trade for horses. Without horses, the Corps of Discovery might not make it across the Rocky Mountains.

Word to Know

INTERPRETER: A person who puts words in one language into another language

Lewis and Clark meet Charbonneau at Fort Mandan.

In February 1805, Sacagawea gave birth to Jean Baptiste Charbonneau. Captain Clark nicknamed him "Pompey." When the Corps left in April, it had 33 crew members, including Charbonneau, Sacagawea, Pompey, and one large dog.

The Corps of Discovery traveled in boats.

In His Own Words

"The sight of this Indian woman … confirmed those people of our friendly intentions, as no woman ever accompanies a war party of Indians in this quarter."
—*Captain Clark, October 19, 1805*

That's a Fact! Seeing Sacagawea and Pompey in the group, Native Americans understood that the expedition was a peaceful mission.

Quick Thinking

Sacagawea's language skills were important to the mission, but it wasn't long before she helped the Corps in other ways, too. One day, high winds tipped one of the boats. Water poured in, soaking important items. Sacagawea fished journals, compasses, books, clothing, and other valuable supplies out of the water. It took three days for everything to dry. In his journal, Captain Clark noted Sacagawea's calm, quick thinking.

Lewis and Clark's pocket compass

In His Own Words

"The Indian woman ... pointed to the gap through which she said we must pass."
—*Captain Clark, 1806*

Pages from Clark's journals

Miles and Miles

The Corps traveled west, 15 to 20 miles a day, toward the mountains through what is today North Dakota and Montana. Sacagawea often walked the muddy river banks with Captain Clark. She might have carried the baby in a Native American cradleboard on her back, or perhaps she made a sling out of cloth to carry him. Along the way, Sacagawea collected food such as wild artichokes, prairie turnips, and berries.

Word to Know

CRADLEBOARD: A wooden baby carrier used by Native Americans

That's a Fact! The Corps of Discovery collected items like rock samples, a buffalo hair ball, and a sheep horn.

A Southwestern cradleboard

The Corps had to travel up the Missouri River on its way to the Pacific Ocean.

Finding the Shoshoni

After months of traveling, Sacagawea recognized the area where the Shoshoni would be hunting buffalo in summer. She pointed it out to the Corps. Soon Captain Lewis met with the Shoshoni chief about trading for horses.

When Captain Lewis asked Sacagawea to be the interpreter for the meeting, she realized that the chief was her brother, Cameahwait (Ca-ME-uh-wate). After a tearful reunion, he told her that most of their family was gone. Sacagawea was overjoyed to find her brother but saddened to hear about her family.

Sacagawea introduces her brother to her son.

To the West

Sacagawea left her brother and headed west with the Corps. Crossing the Rocky Mountains meant day after day of walking across rough land, exhaustion, bitter cold, and very little food.

When they finally neared the Pacific coast, Captain Lewis carved his name and the date into a tree. They had reached their goal.

Now they faced another long winter before they could return East. One day, Lewis and Clark went to see a whale carcass on the beach. Sacagawea wanted to see it, too. There she saw the ocean for the first time. She called it the "big lake."

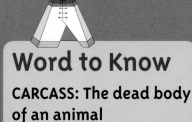

Word to Know

CARCASS: The dead body of an animal

The Pacific Ocean

Mission Complete

During the long journey eastward, the Corps returned Sacagawea, Pompey, and Charbonneau to their home. Then the rest of the Corps continued east.

They had mapped unknown western land, rivers, and mountains. They brought back stacks of journals filled with details about Native Americans. They brought back scientific notes about hundreds of plants and animals they had never seen before. They brought back Native American artifacts. They also brought back lots of stories. Stories of their adventures made other Americans dream about heading out West.

Word to Know

ARTIFACT: A handmade object or tool

A page of notes about a plant collected by Lewis and Clark

Pompey traveled with the Corps from the age of 2 months to 19 months.

Captain Clark knew Sacagawea had been an important member of the Corps. To thank her, he offered to educate her son. The captain had enjoyed many nights around the campfire with the smiling baby. He wanted Pompey to have a good life and a good education. When Pompey was old enough for school, Sacagawea brought him to live with Captain Clark. The boy learned to speak four languages. He later spent years in Europe before returning to America.

That's a Fact!

In the year following the return of the Corps of Discovery, Sacagawea had a daughter named Lizette.

8 Cool Facts About Sacagawea

1 No one knows for sure what Sacagawea's name was as a Shoshoni girl.

2 As a child, Sacagawea probably sewed antelope-skin dolls and dressed them in clothes like those she wore, decorated with colorful beads.

3 During the expedition, Lewis and Clark often described Sacagawea in their journals as strong and patient.

4 Sacagawea appeared on a U.S. coin before Lewis or Clark did.

5

Lewis and Clark referred to Sacagawea as the "Interpreter's Wife" and the "Indian Woman."

6

In the Hidatsa language, Sacagawea's name means "Bird Woman."

7

HISTORY
OF
THE EXPEDITION
UNDER THE COMMAND OF
CAPTAINS LEWIS AND CLARK,
TO
THE SOURCES OF THE MISSOURI,
THENCE
ACROSS THE ROCKY MOUNTAINS
AND DOWN THE
RIVER COLUMBIA TO THE PACIFIC OCEAN.
PERFORMED DURING THE YEARS 1804—5—6.
By order of the
THE UNITED STATES.

When Lewis and Clark's book was published, the publisher spelled Sacagawea with a *j* instead of a *g*, leading people to mispronounce her name.

8

Shoshoni children like Sacagawea counted their age by how many winters they had lived.

Her Final Years

During her lifetime, Sacagawea was not well known. No images of her exist. Most historians believe she died in her 20s in South Dakota. Others believe she lived into her 80s and died in Wyoming.

After the expedition, Sacagawea became well known when an author wrote about her based on interviews with Captain Clark. The author asked lots of questions about the "Indian Woman."

Even today, people are still interested in Sacagawea's story.

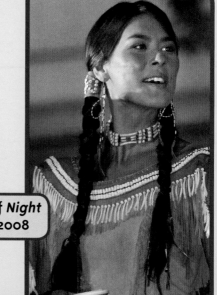

Actress on the set of *Night at the Museum 2*, 2008

Needlepoint, 1930s

Reenactment, 2006

Postage stamp, 1994

39

In Honor of Sacagawea

In the years following the Corps of Discovery's journey, Sacagawea became known as a heroine. She was the strong, smart woman who helped the expedition.

That's a Fact! You can visit a monument in Sacagawea's honor near her birthplace in what is now Salmon, Idaho.

Sacagawea memorial, Salmon, Idaho

All over the United States, statues, monuments, memorials, parks, mountain peaks, schools, and other landmarks celebrate her courage and her role in American history.

Word to Know

MEMORIAL: Something created to remind people of a person, event, or important idea

People in Washington State named this rock Sacagawea and Papoose Rock to honor Sacagawea.

Fact or Fiction?

Many historians disagree about the facts of Sacagawea's life—from the spelling and pronunciation of her name to where, when, and how she died.

Almost everything we know about her life comes from journals, diaries, and notes of members of the expedition. One thing we know for sure is that Sacagawea was a respected member of the Corps of Discovery. She was a true American explorer.

1790
Historians believe Sacagawea was born around this year.

1800
Sacagawea is kidnapped by a Hidatsa war party.

1803
President Thomas Jefferson plans an expedition to the Pacific Ocean.

1804
The Corps of Discovery sets off up the Missouri River.

An illustration of Sacagawea and Pompey

1805

Sacagawea gives birth to Jean Baptiste Charbonneau; she, her husband, and their infant son join the Corps of Discovery.

1806

The Corps of Discovery returns East.

1812

Sacagawea's death is recorded in South Dakota.

2000

The United States honors Sacagawea on a U.S. dollar coin.

Be a Quiz Whiz!

How much do you know about Sacagawea? After reading this book, probably a lot! Take this quiz and find out.

Answers are at the bottom of page 45.

1 Shoshoni Indians moved around a lot in search of:
A. Horses
B. Food
C. Shelter
D. Good weather

2 When she was about ten years old, Sacagawea was:
A. Kidnapped
B. In the fifth grade
C. Winner of a spelling bee
D. Taught to braid hair

3 In the Knife River Villages, Sacagawea learned:
A. To drive a car
B. To shop in a grocery store
C. To grow corn, beans, and squash
D. To read and write

4

In the Hidatsa language, Sacagawea means:
A. Otter Woman
B. Fur Trader's Wife
C. Bird Woman
D. Most Popular

Once Sacagawea saved Lewis and Clark's tools by:
A. Chasing away a grizzly bear
B. Hiding them from attackers
C. Putting them in a safe
D. Fishing them out of the river

5

6

In order to cross the Rocky Mountains, Lewis and Clark needed Sacagawea's help to get:
A. Prairie turnips
B. Horses
C. Gold
D. Buffalo skins

When the Corps met with the Shoshoni Indians, Sacagawea realized the chief was:
A. Her father
B. Her son
C. Her brother
D. Her school teacher

7

Glossary

ACRE: A large unit of land (43,560 square feet)

CORPS: A group of people working together

CRADLEBOARD: A wooden baby carrier used by Native Americans

INTERPRETER: A person who puts words in one language into another language

MEMORIAL: Something created to remind people of a person, event, or important idea

ARTIFACT: A handmade object or tool

CARCASS: The dead body of an animal

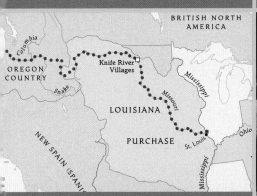

EXPEDITION: A long journey

HISTORIAN: A person who studies history

NOMADIC: Moving around in search of food

PIROGUE: A small wooden boat

Index

Bold page numbers indicate
illustrations.

A
Artifacts 32, 47, **47**

B
Beads 13, 36
Buffalo skins **8,** 9

C
Cameahwait (Shoshoni chief) 28, **29**
Charbonneau, Jean Baptiste
        ("Pompey") 22, 26, **29,** 32,
        34, 35, **40,** 43, **43**
Charbonneau, Toussaint 13, 20, **20–
        21,** 22, 32, 43
Clark, William 16, **16,** 20, **20–21,**
        22–26, 35–38, **36**
Corps of Discovery 14–17, 20–32,
        40, 42, 43
Cradleboards 26, **26,** 46, **46**

D
Dollar coin **36,** 43

F
Fort Mandan 17, **20–21**

H
Hidatsa people
        homes 9, **9, 11**
        language 37
        war party 8, 42
        warriors 8, **8**

J
Jefferson, Thomas 14, **14,** 15, 19, **19,**
        42

K
Knife River Villages 9–10, 17

L
Lewis, Meriwether 16, **16,** 20, **20–
        21,** 28, 30, 36, 36, 37
Lewis and Clark expedition
        boats 16, 22, 24
        interpreter 20, 28
        journals 24, **25,** 32, **33**
        pocket compass **24**
        route map 15
Louisiana Purchase 15

M
Missouri River 27, 42

P
Pacific Ocean 27, 31, **31,** 42
Pirogues 16, 47, **47**

R
Rocky Mountains 6, 15, 20, 30

S
Sacagawea
        birth 6, 42
        childhood 6, 8–10, 36
        death 38, 42, 43
        as interpreter 20, 28
        kidnapping of 8, 42
        monuments and memorials **40,** 41,
                41
        name meaning 37
        U.S. coin **36,** 43
Shoshoni people
        children 37
        food 6, 7
        hunting 6, 28
        language 20

T
Time line 42–43
Toys and dolls 19, **19,** 36, **36**
Traders **12,** 13